WHEN YOU PRAY WITH
YOUNG PEOPLE

WHEN YOU PRAY WITH YOUNG PEOPLE

CONTRIBUTORS

Bryan George
Christopher Gillham
Monica Guiry
Alan Lowe
Paul Montacute
Terry Oakley
Harry Undy
Sarah Williams

Cover design by Anne Farncombe

Published by:
National Christian Education Council
Robert Denholm House
Nutfield,
Redhill, RH1 4HW

British Library Cataloguing-in-Publication Data:
When you pray with young people.
  1. Prayer-books
  I. National Christian Education Council
  291.4'3   BV245

ISBN 0-7197-0566-5

Printed in Great Britain at the University Press, Cambridge

FOREWORD

The prayers in this book have been written for leaders to use with young people from eleven years upwards, and for young people to use in their own meditations.

The prayers are grouped in themes including, the Christian year, the church, everyday living, our family, our work, enjoyment, world crisis, possessions, the media, education and suffering.

CONTENTS

Foreword

The Christian Year	1–18
The Church	19–31
The Bible and literature	32–42
Friends	43–52
Our family: parents and close relations	53–65
Our work:	
Commerce and industry	
Searching for work	66–83
Unemployment	
Enjoyment: Holidays and sport	84–92
Living (distinct from families)	93–109
World Crisis: Justice and peace	110–117
The Media: News, television and radio	118–130
Possessions	131–138
Education: College and university	139–153
Suffering	154–172

Index

THE CHRISTIAN YEAR

ADVENT

1   *Shops have been full of Christmas fare for months. The 'telly' has been bombarding us with suggested gifts.*

Father God, the time has now arrived to begin our spiritual preparation. May we get our priorities right and be able to celebrate Christ's birth worthily.

We recall how you sent John the Baptist to prepare the way; how he commanded the people to demonstrate the faith in their daily lives. Help us to do the same, to make a fresh start at the beginning of the Christian year.

We ask this so that our daily lives reflect the love we profess in worship and celebration. We ask as always in the name of Jesus Christ.

CHRISTMAS

2   Eternal God, you so loved the world you sent Jesus. We thank you again at Christmas-tide for his coming into the world. For the way he came, as a babe in Bethlehem's manger. We cannot visit as did the shepherds and wise men. But we praise you that we can approach him in humility and offer our praise and gratitude in worship.

This we do gladly and reverently.

3   We recall the journey of the Magi. We wonder if
they were surprised when at the end of the road,
they saw the light of the star, illuminating
not a grand palace, but a stable adjoining the
local inn. May this constantly remind us that
Christ can be found in the most unlikely places.
That his presence is not restricted to church
and chapel. Help us to seek and find him in every
situation, offering our best gifts just as the wise men
presented their gold, frankincense and myrrh.

4   *It is suggested that the following prayer might
be used in personal devotions on Christmas Day.*

'Love came down at Christmas
Love all lovely, love divine . . .'

Lord Jesus Christ, help me to love like you.
You said I should love God and love my neighbour
as myself. Today I want to show my willingness
to be obedient as I pray for people for whom you
have special concern.

5   Here at home, surrounded by family and friends, I
think of young people inadequately housed in bed-and-
breakfast accommodation.
Of others, who roam the streets of the large cities,
sleeping between cardboard boxes on pavements in
doorways and subways.
Some have quarrelled with parents, others have been
unable to maintain human relationships and are conse-
quently lonely, feel rejected and unwanted.

6   As I enjoy good things to eat and drink, I remember those dependent upon charity, victims of famine, some even dying at this time through malnutrition.

This holiday-time, the opportunity for rest and recreation prompts me to commend to your care all who are too tired to enjoy the break from life's routine.

I pray too for those who must work during this festival, maintaining emergency services, caring for the sick, for those whose work makes possible our celebrations.

We thank you for health and strength; be near to those who are ill or handicapped, alcoholic or drug-addicts. Comfort relatives and friends who anxiously watch as their loved-ones suffer.

Father we ask these things in your name.

NEW YEAR

7   At the beginning of another year, we ask you Heavenly Father to:

> accept our gratitude for the way in which you have provided for us in the past. Grant your forgiveness for all those silly and selfish things that have caused hurt to others, ourselves and to you.

> Hear our prayer as we seek courage and strength to confidently face the unknown, believing that you work for good in the lives of those who love you.

8 As we embark upon the next stage of life's
journey we place our trust in you, knowing that
with your assistance we can keep our resolutions,
honour our vows, be diligent in prayer and
Bible study and be faithful members of your church.

We ask, as always, in the name of Jesus Christ, your
Son.

LENT

9 Lord Jesus,
you were tempted.
You know how hard it is to stand firm and not sin.
Thank you for your example.
When the power of temptation seems too great,
help us never to be too proud to run away;
creating the greatest possible distance between
us and the scene of testing in the shortest
possible time.
Thank you for occasions of temptation. We know
that when by your grace we are able to stand
firm, we are better Christians for the experience.
More able to be victorious in the future.
But Lord, when we fail, forgive us.

PASSIONTIDE

10 *Let us meditate on the reactions of Jesus to both friends and
enemies during the last days of his earthly life.*

On Palm Sunday, Jesus, aware that entering Jerusalem would lead to arrest, declined to enter secretly but rode in triumph acknowledging the acclamation of the crowd. Selflessly he offers his people one last chance to recognise and respond to his Messiahship

> Help me, Father, to be like Jesus. Selfless,
> courageous, more concerned with others than
> with personal comfort and safety.

Following his protests in the Temple, Jesus was approached by enemies who tried to discredit him with unanswerable questions. He was too clever for them.

> Grant, Father, that the indwelling of the
> Holy Spirit may enable me, through thoughtful
> study give a good account of my faith.

In the Garden of Gethsemane Jesus spent time in prayer, gaining the necessary strength to face the difficulties ahead.

> At times of crisis in my life, help me to
> prepare myself spiritually. Like my master,
> may I be able finally to say . . . 'Not my will,
> but thy will be done!'

When Jesus went to the Upper Room to have a last meal with his disciples, he discovered them quarrelling among themselves over questions of seniority. He responded by adopting the role of the servant and washing their feet.

> Lord Jesus, when I quarrel or walk out slamming
> the door in a temper! Teach me a better way.

On the Cross, after looking down upon those responsible for the cruel suffering he was enduring, our Lord looked towards heaven and prayed . . .

'Father, forgive, they know not what they do.'

Father God, help me to love and forgive like Jesus.

EASTER

11 Almighty God, like Paul we thank you for 'giving us the victory by the resurrection of Jesus Christ our Lord.'
We praise you for what you have done,
   turning sorrow into joy,
   evil into good,
   defeat into victory,
   death into life!
We are happy because we have a living Saviour. We may not fully understand the miracle of resurrection, but we know that Jesus who died on the cross, conquered death and is alive for ever.

12 Grant Father God, that just as Jesus appeared to the disciples in the Upper Room, he may come to us as we gather for worship; that as he journeyed with Cleopas and his friend on the way to Emmaus, he may be with us as we travel life's road.
And if like Thomas we find real difficulty in believing, or like Peter embarrassed because of recent sins, we ask for a special visitation to banish our doubts and assure us of your forgiving love.

ASCENSION

13 Lord Jesus Christ, we are grateful, that having completed the work you came to earth to do, you returned to heaven in glory.
We praise you that your presence is not restricted. That you are able to be with all people at all times and in all places.
So often we fail to complete the task begun.
We give up when we encounter difficulty or hardship. Forgive our weakness and help us to follow your example more closely.

'Go ye into all the world, preaching, teaching and baptising' you said to your disciples. We pray for men and women who have been obedient to that command.

'And lo, I will be with you always . . . ' Be with us in every activity of our lives.

PENTECOST

14 Father, Jesus promised to send the Holy Spirit. Today we celebrate the coming into the world of the Spirit.

Jesus said that the Spirit would . . .
> open our eyes to the truth,
> strengthen our wills,
> guide us in times of uncertainty,
> befriend us when we are lonely.

Help us day by day to rely upon the Holy Spirit!
He also said that the Spirit would . . .
> increase our understanding of the Bible,
> guide us in times of prayer,
> inspire us when we worship.

Help us day by day to rely upon the Holy Spirit!

15 Today is the birthday of the Church. Thank you for the local fellowship to which we belong and the great company of believers scattered throughout this world. We look back with gratitude and forward with hope.

16 May your Holy Spirit dwell with us, that we may make a worthy contribution to the life and witness of your church and play our part in extending your rule among mankind.

HARVEST

17   Almighty God, in the beginning you created the world, for men and women to live in it and enjoy it. Down through the years you have provided for all our children's needs. We thank you for your providential care.

Lord, forgive the way we spoil things through thoughtlessness, selfishness and greed. We waste precious resources, we live as if there is no tomorrow, we misuse so many of your gifts. May we never take your kindness for granted. Make us responsible stewards of abilities and possessions. At this season of the year we thank you for food and clothing. Forgive us for considering as necessities many of your gifts which in other parts of the world are thought of as luxuries.
Enable us to follow more closely the example of Jesus, and so live our lives that more of your children will find life purposeful and worthwhile.

REMEMBRANCE DAY

18   Father,
following the two minutes silence we hear
those words again . . . 'They shall not grow
old as we that are left to grow old, age shall
not weary them, nor the years condemn. At
the going down of the sun and in the morning
we will remember them . . .'

But, I cannot remember them; it all happened so
long ago.
I cannot understand why faces are still sad and
the eyes of the elderly so full of tears.
Father help me to be compassionate and understanding, and forgive my insensitivity.

THE CHURCH

THE CHURCH

19 *'All of you are Christ's Body' 1 Corinthians 12.27*

It sounds great—in theory.
All the different parts
working as one.
But the reality is different.
Look at the body of the Church . . .
old separated from young;
Catholic from Protestant;
white from black;
happy-clappy praisers from dead serious mourners.
Is this the body I belong to?
Look at the body in the mirror . . .
Is that me . . . that hair
that nose . . . that skin?
What happens to the hopes, the ideals
when they need feet and hands to make them real?
Is this body me?

God! It's amazing!
How could you love such a body as this?
How could you allow this to be your body?
Help me look again, and see what you see.
Help me be myself, as you want me to be.
Help me to be part of the Church,
in all its peculiarities.
Help me to be . . .
your body.

COMMITTED CHURCH

20   *To be used before baptism, confirmation or being received into full membership or before a Covenant Service.*

Lord,
if being part of the Church
means being committed to you,
and acknowledging your commitment to me,
then I want to be part of the Church.

Lord,
if being a member of the Church
means standing alongside the oppressed,
committed to the cause of justice and peace,
discovering you, present in the poor,
then I want to be a member of the Church.

Lord,
if being in the Church
means being identified as one who follows you
and recognised as someone who tries to live in your
way,
then I want to be in the Church.

Lord,
if the Church betrays its commitment to you,
loses its way and shows itself flawed and sinful,
then forgive and reclaim it.

Lord,
I confess my share of failure, and my need for help.
Help me to see that the Church always needs
reforming, and may my commitment to you
keep me faithful also to your Church.

BAPTISM

21   *For those baptised as infants.*

It wasn't my choice. I don't remember it.
It had nothing to do with me!
No, it was other people who decided.
Yet, others who cared enough, believed enough,
did enough, to bring me towards baptism.
Who were they?

Parents—who for all their obvious faults,
for all their compromised faith,
yet, for me, chose Christ.

Church—the people who welcomed me in Christ's
name, who promised me their love, their care, their
support, who willingly accepted me as I was,
even though I had done nothing to deserve their love.

And you Lord? Present at my baptism?
Yes, and still present, receiving me,
leading me, filling me with your Spirit.

22   God, you are often addressed as a parent,
forgive our parents when they force us to live
with the consequences of their actions,
even when taken in good faith;
and help us to be thankful for the start they gave us.

God, Spirit of peace and reconciliation,
forgive me for my pride in thinking that what I do
matters most. Help me continue growing in faith,
responding in hope, and testifying in love.

23 *For those baptised as believers.*

It was my choice, but your call;
it was my witness, but your grace;
it was my faith, but your death.

No, it wasn't all me!
There were those who cared enough, believed enough
did enough to bring me towards baptism.
Who?

Parents and friends—famous and ordinary people,
all those who showed me Christ, and told the Gospel.

You Lord? Present at my baptism?
Yes, you, much more vital than the water,
the words, the music, or the feelings.
Your love offered first, before it all,
through it all, and it always will be.

Forgive me, when I claim too much for myself;
help me to speak thankfully of your action in my life.

24 By the waters of baptism,
a sign is given,
a truth declared,
a life is offered in Christ.
Forgive us for diluting the power of baptism,
by mixing it with apathy, custom, or superstition;
renew us with your Spirit, send us with your Word
and fill us with your love.

COMMUNION

25 We come by invitation, not by right;
we come to receive, not to buy;
we come together, not alone;
we come to share, not to claim.

We are one, united, reconciled, forgiven
healed and made whole.
In solidarity with all who confess Christ
we become the community of bread and wine.
In union with Christ, we become the children of God.

Lord, receive us, reconcile us and renew us.
Bless the Lord of love;
Bless the God of grace;
Bless the Spirit of peace.

WORSHIPPING CHURCH

26 *A prayer to prepare for worship.*

Listen to your pulse, your heart beat.
Breathe slowly, steadily . . .

Here I am.
Ready.
Breathing in . . . life-giving air,
breathing out. . . life-giving air.
Into . . . God's Spirit;
out to . . . God's Spirit.
An exchange of being . . . present in the universe,
In Spirit and in truth.
Here I am
to worship.

MINISTRY

27   *Everyone has a ministry.*

> I'm not sure if I have any gifts.
> What can I do that someone else can't do twice
> as well?
> I'd only make a mess of things.
> They'd be silly to rely on me.
> I've tried, but I'm not good enough.
> I can't speak out in public;
> I'm not musical or artistic;
> I can't read well, or give a moving testimony.
> I can't really be a Christian, can I?

'Do you love me?'

Yes, Lord, you know I love you.

'Love, is the greatest gift.
Love as I have loved you.'

HOUSE CHURCH

28   *Can be used when in the setting of a home.*

This is how it was at first . . .
meeting together in someone's house,
sharing hospitality, friendship and faith,
in the name of Jesus.
It reminds us that the Church stretches back
through the centuries:
one home to another,
one meal to another,
one prayer to another,
one disciple to another,
in continuous succession.

WITNESSES

29   If anyone asks, can we tell them?
If someone is seeking, will we be able to point the way?
If they cross-question us, will our evidence remain
credible?

Lord, our mission is to witness for you!
to direct people's attention towards your love;
to share the Good News that brings hope;
to live so that your glory is seen,
and the kingdom is glimpsed.
Help us to be ready,
humble, clear and convincing.

LISTENING CHURCH

30   How can we proclaim, unless we have first listened?
Lord, we need to hear your word, spoken for today.
We need to look for your acts, performed in the
present.
We need to be open to your Spirit, changing our ways.
We need to be a listening Church.
Speak, Lord, as we listen.

UNITY

31   *May be used in the Week of Prayer for Christian Unity, or
when young people from different churches are sharing in a
joint activity or event.*

Unity is not about being the same, thank goodness!
We're different—and proud to be.
Still, its good to discover we share
some things in common, especially
our search for God, our looking to Jesus.
Our fellowship in the Spirit.

THE BIBLE AND LITERATURE

A GOOD BOOK

32 How kind you are, O God, to give us so many worlds. As we sit with a book, we can leave our lives and follow great adventures in strange lands. We can become entwined with the characters, knowing them as friends. We can live their lives with ours. We praise you for the gift of imagination which allows authors to invent so many wonderful worlds for our delight.

THE GOOD BOOK

33 *John 21.25*

As we step into a library, we enter a world full of excitement and adventure; of imagination and information. In books, we can find facts about every subject. But there is one book which is a library in itself. In its pages, one can find romance and heroism, poetry and history, philosophy and law. It contains facts about every subject, for it is not restricted to our world.

It is the story of God and the story of life; the story of creation and the story of salvation. It is our hope and our assurance. It tells of God's love and his promise to man. It is the book above all books. May God be blessed for his message of love to mankind.

THE LAW

34 *Mark 12.29-31*

Dear Lord, there are many people who use the Bible even though they do not know it. There are some who remember only three words, 'Thou shalt not', and use them to reinforce all their prejudices. They forget that, in Jesus, you superseded the law. His laws are not negative. He gives two great positive commandments which sum up the entire law. Help us to be truly law abiding; to love you, our God, with all our being and to love our neighbours as ourselves.

THE PROPHETS

35 *Isaiah 6.8 & 9 Jeremiah 1.4-10*

'Here am I, Lord, send me.' Whether we have the wonderful confidence of Isaiah or the diffidence of Jeremiah, we know, Lord that you can use anyone. Make us ready to be sent. Fill us with the faith of the Prophets. Let us know your will as they knew it and let us obey as they obeyed.

THE PREACHER

36 *Ecclesiastes 1 & 2 (or the whole book)*

What a brave person the Preacher must have been allowing his mind to wander over every sorrow, every enigma of mankind. What courage to stand and proclaim a philosophy of emptiness; to look at all mankind's activities and to find them in vain. How near to despair one must have come!

The preacher cries to our century as it rushes after material wealth. Have we been this way before? You alone, Almighty God, are lasting. You alone, give hope. The Preacher grasps at that hope, we find it in Jesus.

We praise you for a hope fulfilled and we praise you for a mighty philosopher who went in search of it.

THE HISTORIES

37 *Judges 6-8*

Lord God of Abraham and of Isaac and of Jacob: many have called you by that name. It is strange that the history of one nation should form part of scripture. It is just an ordinary history with its fair share of rogues, but through it, you have taught us so much. You have shown that sinful people can be forgiven and do your work. You have shown that ordinary people like Gideon can be singled out to become great in your service.

You have shown that you understand our fears and will give proofs of your presence. May we be as ready as they to accept the proofs and become your agents.

THE GOSPELS

38 *Luke 2.1-7 & Luke 23.26-48*

From the manger in Bethlehem to the cross at Golgotha, the message is the same: the story of selfless sacrifice. Jesus, God incarnate, giving himself to win victory for heedless, sinful man.

How we bless you, Almighty Creator, for the constant love that we know through Jesus.

THE PSALMS

39   *Psalm 150*

David sang in ecstasy before you, his Great God.
We read his songs in solemn tones. But we can sing too.
Fill our hearts with the ecstasy of music, that we may
make a joyful sound unto the Lord.

THE APOSTLES

40   *Acts 2*

Eleven frightened men, hiding, confused. One saw
and believed. One proclaimed, 'My Lord and My God!'

Eleven joyful men, wondering how they could tell
the world.

The Holy Spirit was given.

Eleven confident men told the world.

Oh Holy Spirit, guide our lives that we may serve as
gladly, as confidently and as constantly as they.

THE EPISTLES

41   *1 Corinthians 13*

He wrote and wrote, a man full of energy, eager to
explain and to encourage. To wipe out false teachings.

In his letters, he developed all sorts of doctrines, but he
knew, none better, the whole duty of a Christian; to
love.

May we learn love and practise it all our lives
through.

THE WORD

42   *John 1.1-5*

Pre-existent. Ever present. Never ending.
All glorious. All powerful. All creating.

In pity, you came to earth for us. In compassion, you gave yourself for us. In mercy, you died for us. Word of God incarnate, we praise you. We worship you. We love you. Bless us now and always with your constant presence.

FRIENDS

FAITHFUL FRIENDS

43   You knew what it was like, Lord,
to be let down,
deserted,
betrayed
by your own friends.

You knew what it was like, Lord,
to be afraid of being
rejected,
ridiculed
by your public.

You knew what it was like, Lord,
to be hurt,
battered,
condemned
by the authorities.

You know.
You understand.
You remain faithful.
You keep encouraging.
You heal our hurts.

Let your loyalty and sacrifice
be our inspiration;
and as your friends
help us to be faithful
to our friends and to you.

CLOSE FRIENDS

44   *Use this when there has been a sharing of personal experiences, and an atmosphere of close community.*

John 11.5,13.23

Having friends close-by is good.
But,
too close . . .
and it becomes embarrassing.
They can see what I really am like,
and bluff and bluster can't hide -
the real me,
unsure, wanting to be reassured;
self-conscious, wanting to know I'm accepted.

That's when close friends can help me:

to relax and be myself,
without worrying;
to ask the silly question,
and be given an answer
- or know we both don't know;
to share a secret that has been a burden,
and know that its safe;
to test out the dreams and dares
and find how to bring them to reality;
to bear their trust,
and be strong for them;
to help too, by listening and supporting
as they search and quest.

Lord, thank you for my close friends,
who let me discover who I really am.
Lord, thank you for the example of your close friendships, with John and Lazarus, Mary and Martha.

'JUST FRIENDS'

45 *Use this when discussing relationships between the sexes. Much will depend on the level of confidence built up within the group as to how great a sharing there can be.*

'We're just friends', I told them.
Then felt as if I'd betrayed my loyalty.
My friend, Lord, is of the opposite sex,
which makes things so difficult.
It makes it hard to know when friendship ends
and something . . . more begins.
It makes it hard to decide which friendships are more
important, with those of my own sex, or this one.
My friend is very special.
Kind and thoughtful, yes; understanding, too.
Good fun to be with, and . . . attractive.
Being together is exciting.
I want it to be more than 'just friends',
but I'm scared of what the others will say.
What do I do, Lord?
Help me to be faithful to all my friends, girls and boys.

ABSENT FRIENDS

46 *Spend some time thinking of absent friends.*

'I feel so alone.
My friend has gone.'

Lord, we pray for our friends who are a long way away . . .; those who are in other countries . . .; those in different cities, towns or villages. Be with them, and bless them.

47   Lord, we pray for our friends who are not here because of illness . . .; those in hospital, or at home . . .; those in pain, or housebound by disability. Be with them, and bless them.

48   Lord, we pray for our friends who are estranged from us . . .; those with whom we have argued . . .; those we have offended, or hurt or neglected. Be with them, and help us to seek their forgiveness.

49   Lord, we remember our friends who have died . . .; those whose deaths still grieve us . . .; those who are remembered with deep affection . . .; those whom we have begun to forget.

Accept our thanks for their lives, and bless those who feel their loss.

Lord, we pray that we may be present as a friend in time of need, as you are the ever-present friend for us.

FASCINATING FRIENDS

50   Thank you for our friends who lead such exciting and fascinating lives.

Thank you for friends who have travelled in many countries and for the wonderful and strange stories they tell.

Thank you for friends who have exciting jobs, meeting the famous; facing danger; and for the glamour they bring into our lives.

Thank you for friends with special interests, hobbies and past-times, and for their enthusiasm which helps us share in their enjoyment.

Thank you for friends who have the courage to be different, and who show us how varied life can be, and the importance of each unique individual.

Thank you for friends with a great sense of humour, for the laughter they share with us, and for helping us to appreciate our own sense of the funny and ridiculous.

Thank you for friends who have deep faith in you, which makes their lives so special; for their witness to you; their love to other people, and their hope in the future.

FORGIVING FRIENDS

51   *Read the first part, then after a few moments silence read the second. See Matthew 18.21,22 (or 10-35)*

They forgave me . . .
though I'd hurt them so much,
though I'd done it deliberately, knowingly,
wanting them to feel the pain,
because I felt jealous, angry and lonely.
Afterwards, I was ashamed, guilty and sorry.
But it was too late, so I thought.
But they still wanted me to be their friend.
They felt so much for me they forgave me.
They are still my friends.

I must forgive them . . .
though they've embarrassed me, making me look a fool, though they've been cruel, leaving me on my own.
They have lots of love and kindness.
Now they will feel regret.
It will be hard for them to speak to me,
or live with themselves.
I will forgive them; show them I want them,
and need them as my friends.

FORGIVING FRIENDS

52   *Read the first part, then after a few moments silence read
the second. See Matthew 18.21,22 (or 10-35)*

She forgave me . . .
though I'd hurt her so much,,
though I'd done it deliberately,
wanting her to feel the pain,
because I felt jealous, angry and lonely.
Afterwards, I was ashamed,
and regretted what I'd done.
But it was too late, so I thought.
But she still wanted me to be her friend.
She felt so much for me she forgave me.
She is still my friend.

I must forgive him . . .
though he's embarrassed me, making me look a fool,
though he's been cruel, leaving me on my own.
He has lots of love and kindness.
Now he will feel regret.
It will be hard for him to speak to me,
or live with himself.
I will forgive him; show him I want him,
and need him as my friend . . . 'I Forgive you'

OUR FAMILY

TRADING IN

53   'Here are my mother and my brothers!' said Jesus.
'Whoever does God's will is my brother, sister, mother.'

His welcome cuts deep into my heart.

Who is my brother, my sister, my mother?
Are they my family by design or mistake?

'I didn't choose them!' I cry,
'I didn't ask to be born'.
Today I could cheerfully walk out for good.
I feel betrayed by their closeness their mocking and their jokes as if they'd prefer to trade me in for something else.

'Here are my mother and my brothers' said Jesus.
Knowing he'd soon be traded in, Saviour for political leader.

Oh Jesus, help me, my Brother to welcome and cherish, forgive and to love as you do.

54   Give us the courage to do what's right
when everything looks wrong.
Give us, Lord, the wisdom
when the day seems very long.
To put things right,
before the night,
and be at peace with Thee.

UNHAPPY FAMILIES

55 Lord God,
Your children are not very good at loving one another.
We love conditionally and put up our defences when
things go wrong.
When things do go wrong, we like to find a culprit
- someone to blame.
Lord, teach us that marriages are not 'made in Heaven'
and then handed to us, and when mistakes are made let
us not seek out the guilty party, but seek to forgive and
be forgiven.

56 We pray for those who suffer because of an unhappy
marriage. We pray for adults who are going through the
traumas of separation and divorce; for children who are
being torn in different directions and wonder if they are
still being loved; for other family members who may be
shattered and distressed. Help them to continue to love
and support without attaching blame. We pray particularly for those we know, maybe within our own family,
who have been witnessing a break-up of their home.
We ask that you might aid the healing of their wounds,
and be a source of comfort and encouragement to them.

57 Teach us all, Lord God, not to withhold our love for
fear of being hurt. May our love be honest and without
condemnation, even though we may not always understand the 'whys' and the 'wherefores'.
We ask this in the name of our Father who is the Lord
God.

INTERCESSIONS

58   Our Father in Heaven, we look to you because you hold us in perfect love.
You know our needs better than we ourselves.
We pray for our parents, and others who have shouldered responsibility for bringing us up.
Thank you for the sacrifices they have made for us.
Thank you for the love of a parent for a child.

Short time of silence to bring personal, specific requests to God.

Abba, Father, hear the prayers of your children

We pray for brothers and sisters with whom we have shared our growing up. They have known us at our best and at our worst.
Close or not, they are irreplaceable.
Thank you for all relations who have been special to us, and for their influence upon our lives.
We pray for them.

Short time of silence.

Abba, Father, hear the prayers of your children

We are made to be God's children and as such, we wish to take after our Father.
We pray therefore that we may relate to others with love that treasures each one as special.
We pray for ourselves in all our family relationships, that through them our Father in heaven may be glorified.

Abba, Father, hear the prayers of your children

EXPERIENCES

59 Dear Father,
I pray that in families everywhere, parents may learn wisdom as they bring up their children. That they may be able to remain childlike enough to appreciate their children's needs, loves and joys.

I pray for young people that as they grow up, they might learn how to build loving and trusting relationships. I pray that they might be encouraged to share their youth as they begin to explore adulthood.

Remind us all, Father, that others do not necessarily have the same kind of family experiences as we do, and therefore may we always be open to learning from the experiences of others and free from making false assumptions. Keep everyone young at heart, for the Kingdom of God belongs to such as these.

I'LL KEEP TRYING

60 *After another argument*
(I confess my fault this time)
I lick my wounds and assess the damage.
Nothing worse than hurt pride.
Lord, I tried.
I tried to understand their point of view, and all their reasons 'why', but yet my temper got the better of me.
Their reasons became chains holding me down, their points of view like manacles locking me into place.

What is it about parents?
They're not always right, in fact, they're often wrong.
Yet they even have a way of being wrong that is so reasonable.

My behaviour's not defensible, my charity does not begin at home.
I wouldn't choose my parents as friends but here we are and they choose to stick it out with me.
I must keep trying to understand and because they want to understand me.
Please help me to communicate and let them know why I just don't feel free.

WITH THANKS

61 Heavenly Father,
I would like to thank you for those who are dear to me, especially all my family and relations.
I am glad to have family ties because they are ties of love and caring, not bonds of duty and restriction.
Help me to do my best to be a good relation and to understand my role within the wider family of God.

GOD IS WITH US

62 Whatever it is that goes wrong in human relationships and causes hurt, pain, grief, suffering, you suffer with us. Thank you for your compassion and your understanding. You feel with us every moment of rejection, deceit, sorrow and loss.

FOR MY FAMILY

63   Lord, my friends all keep thick diaries
        I find that hard to do.
    I forget to keep them up to date
        So I'd sooner talk to you.
    I've known you now just eighteen months
        Long enough to find
    That if you don't agree with me
        I really shouldn't mind.
    So when I prayed for my dear friend
        That he/she be healed by you
    I really didn't expect him/her to
        Be well again so soon!
    I'd like to pray for others now,
        my parents and my friends
    And because I might not get it right,
        I'd rather you would share
    Your blessing with each one of them
        According to their needs
    And when you've worked out all of that
        Please spare the rest for me!

TO GO TO THE TRINITY

64   God the Father
    You are the perfect Father. May we learn from you the
    perfect way to live in family love, and be forgiven for
    our imperfect ways.

    God the Son
    You taught us to honour our parents and then showed
    us the honour that took you to the cross. May we, too,
    honour our parents not least when it costs.

God the Holy Spirit
You guide our lives in love and peace. May we depend
upon you to bring love and peace to our family battles,
wholeness and guidance to our family life.

God the Trinity
You are Three in One, the beginning and the end. May
we live together in community, the community of God,
individual and interdependent.
All glory and honour be yours forever more.

HE IS HERE

65   You fill
the gulf between the silently grieving family who have
not spoken to one another for five years.
You are
in the corner with the helpless little baby who has been
beaten black and blue for crying.
You stay
with the struggling single parent, when the one who
'made it all happen' has long since left.
You stand
by the old and the distraught, who, after many shared
years, are expected to cope with the sudden death of a
loving partner.
You are
here with us, as we grapple with the right words of
comfort to offer them.

What can we say now, but 'Thank you' and 'Don't let
us go'. We need you.

OUR WORK

TEENAGE DECISIONS

66   *Because of the uncertainty of the modern world of work,*
teenagers are faced with making difficult choices that could
affect the whole of their lives. Here is a prayer that helps to
put the choices in a divine context but leaves the decision to
the teenager.

Help me Lord,
to decide what I should do,
All my life is still before me.
I must choose which way to go.
I am faced with the choice of staying on at school and
studying.
I am advised that it will improve my working chances.
I must choose what I should do.
I could go for training on some government scheme.
I would then be sure of a brief and steady time before
me.
But what then?
I must decide what I should do.
I could look for a proper job.
I could wait and become unemployed.
This seems so easy. But what shall I become?
I must decide what I should do.
Each choice could lead to nowhere in today's uncertain
world.
But I will choose and go with you, Lord.
You will use whichever way I go!

PRODUCTION

67   *We are made in the image of God. One of the signs of that image is that we are able to create as he created. We share with him the gift of creation.*

Creator God, we thank you for your gift of creation.
We thank you for making us creators in your image.
We thank you for our skill, knowledge and ingenuity.

We thank you for the way your gifts in us and in the world have been brought together over the ages to produce the variety of goods we enjoy.

We thank you for the products of our joint creativity.

CREATOR GOD

68   We thank you for all the goods that make our work in the home easier.

Together we have produced building materials, glass, and steel.

We thank you for all the goods that surround our work in industry and commerce.

Together we have harnessed wind, sea, fire and the atom.

We thank you for all the sources of energy that make our personal strength and energy go further.

Together we have controlled pests, germs and disease.

We thank you for all the chemicals and medicines that make our lives healthier.

69   Dear Jesus, suffering and loving friend, I want you to understand my helplessness and pain.

You had a tradesman's skill; were a carpenter of note.
You gave this up to do your Father's will.
You healed the sick. You taught with skill.
You walked the country paths, the village streets.
You spoke with power. Tired yourself out.
The priestly caste, the ruling powers, put you to death.
The Cross was what you worked for.
Today there is no work.. Today this is my Cross.
How can I share my life with you?

70   Dear Holy Spirit, powerful, ceaseless companion, I want you to understand my anger and frustration.

You came as Holy Spirit, a powerful, driving force that set the world on fire.
You drove men to mighty deeds.
The early church was built up by your power.
Men and women received your restless energy.
They worked with and for you, proclaiming all God's grace.
Mary, Peter, Paul, Augustine, Wycliffe, Luther,
the Wesleys, Florence Nightingale, Mother Theresa,
all found work to do for you.
Today there is no work. But you still have work to do.
Please, may I use my life for you.

FORGIVE US FOR DESTROYING YOUR WORLD

71 *The world of work is all too often bedevilled with selfishness and greed. Man has made his mark on God's world all too often with devastating results. We must frequently remind ourselves of this and ask God's forgiveness.*

Oh great and loving God, Creator and Keeper of all the universe, we come confessing that we have abused your wonderful creation.

We fill the air with poisonous fumes that destroy the trees and ourselves. Our work is choking your world because we want to make more and more money.

We fill the rivers and seas with deadly waste that kills the fish and other forms of life. Our work is drowning your creatures because we won't clean up our own filth as it costs too much.

We strip the land of its trees and natural cover creating waste lands where little of value can survive. Our work consumes irreplaceable materials because of our unsatisfied demands, our selfish greed.

72 We take unthinkingly and uncaring from the riches you have provided and give nothing in return.

Forgive us, O Lord, Our God, and grant us insight and understanding of the delicate balance and inter-related wholeness of your wonderful world.

Through your forgiveness help us to see your world as you created it, and give us the courage, strength and determination to use it wisely for the good of all mankind.

WILLING TO DO GOD'S WORK

73 *Jesus was always ready to do God's will. His work was to show the prevailing love of God for all mankind.*

May I, O Lord, be ever ready and ever willing to do the work you have for me to do.

May I always keep my mind sharp, my strength ready, and my heart open for each moment and each task you present to me.

May I always respond with loving kindness to your call to do your work.

May I never lose sight of the consistent examples set by Jesus.

May my work for you be done through following in Jesus' footsteps.

May my life and the work I do be used to give praise to you, O Lord, my God.

FOR THE WORLD OF WORK

74 O Almighty, Powerful, and yet Loving God, we remind ourselves at this time that the world is yours; that you are still at work in the world; that you have placed us in this world as creatures made in your image; that you have set an example for our daily lives in the life of Jesus of Nazareth who lived in complete obedience to your will; that through your Holy Spirit you have provided us with the strength and energy to become fellow-workers with you; and that the whole world is your work place for the benefit of all mankind.

75   Father, we pray for:
      the unemployed; those who want to work and cannot
      because there is none for them to do; those who would
      like to work but cannot because of ill-health or disabi-
      lity; those who will not work for whatever reason;
          Grant us all a new vision of your working world and
      our part in it.

76   Father, we pray for:
      the workers, those in the dirty, monotonous jobs in
      heavy industry; those in shops and offices who provide
      services for others; those in satisfying jobs who find
      real reward in their work; those whose work regularly
      overwhelms them by its sheer pressure; those who
      work for themselves in the varied contexts of the
      industrial and commercial worlds.
          Grant us all a new vision of your working world and
      our part in it.

77   Father, we pray for:
      the managers, those who struggle to keep conditions as
      pleasant as possible for the workers; those who are
      unable to see the importance of the human side of their
      business; those who are willing to adapt to new devel-
      opments and help the company survive; those who are
      facing difficult financial decisions and threats to their
      workforce.
          Grant us all a new vision of your working world and
      our part in it.

78 Father, we pray for:
the Government; the Chancellor of the Exchequer who controls the financial climate for the working world; the Employment Minister who seeks to create and maintain a climate of steady growth and development; all other Government Ministers whose decisions affect the millions of people involved in the world of work.

Grant us all a new vision of your working world and our part in it.

May your Kingdom grow to embrace all mankind, to your honour and glory.

THE POSITIVE SIDE OF PRODUCTION

79 *In the act of using God's creation many have been able to produce a variety of goods that have increased the comfort of living in the world.*

I thank you, God, that by working in your world mankind has been able to extend the comforts of your creation. I thank you for the production of steel and plastic that we use to make motor cars and new hip-joints. I thank you for the production of the silicon chip which we use to make televisions and heart pace-makers.

I thank you for the production of the laser that we use to carry messages around the world and for eye surgery. I thank you for the production of nuclear energy that provides electricity and cures some cancers.

For the many products we have made from your created order, I thank you, Lord. I pray that we may continue to use the products of our hands and minds fashioned from the materials you have provided, to serve the needs of all your children.

GOD USES THE WEAK

80   You called weak and helpless people to do your work.
You reminded them of their value; that they were
precious to you. They were important to your work
about speaking out about the Good News of your love
for all people.

I pray that you will take my helplessness, my frustration, my energy, my willingness, my commitment,
and use me to build up a small part of your Kingdom
here on earth. For your name's sake.

THE SIMPLEST THINGS BUILD THE NEW
TECHNOLOGY

81   *The more we understand about God's world the more we
realise that all the rich variety of life and its apparent
complexity is built up out of the simplest parts.*

I am amazed at the marvellous way that we have been
able to use the simplest things to make very complicated equipment to work better and faster than we
could do ourselves. There are robots that are able to put
cars together, and they never get bored! There are
computers that work out the most complicated mathematical formulas so quickly we stand amazed. There
are body-scanners that read how the inside of our
bodies are functioning and give us pictures of the
results.

All of these machines and many more are built up on
just two pieces of information, a plus or a minus, an on
or off switch. How wonderful is the world you have
created!

Your might and majesty is built on the working of
the simplest of things. We rejoice in the simple working
of your world.

I pray that we will build all our new technology as a
thanks-offering to you, our Lord and our God.

FOR ALL THOSE INVOLVED IN THE WORLD OF WORK

82 *For the Christian, work is a great responsibility. It is the way in which we can make an on-going contribution to God for all his loving kindness towards us.*

We pray for those caught up in the dull dreariness of repetitive work.

Grant them a glimpse of the full part they play in the act of production.

We pray for those bogged down in the muck and grime of dirty work. Grant them a glimpse of the brightness of the finished product of their labour.

We pray for those who must work when others rest.

Grant them a glimpse of the needs of those they serve.

We pray for those who suffer through industrial injury or disease.

Grant them the satisfaction of their job well done and the necessary grateful support of their employer.

We pray for those who find fulfilment in their work.

Grant them the insight to know that they are blessed.

We pray for those who strive to create new work in a changing world.

Grant them success for the good of those who are out of work.

For all those who make up the rich variety of the world of work, we pray that they may realise their great responsibility to other human beings and to you, their Creator, so that as co-workers with you they may strive to bring about the new kingdom.

THE WORK OF GOD AND OF MAN

83 *Man has contributed to the beauty and wonder of the world. Christians also should give thanks to God for the wonders of creation.*

We give you thanks for the beautiful handiwork of your Creation.

The work of your hands is revealed in the beauty of the rose, the orchid, and the daffodil. Their splendour pleases our eyes.

We thank you for the work of our hands revealed in the beauty of a painting, an illuminated manuscript, and a tapestry. We pray that their splendour pleases your eye, O God.

We thank you for the work of your hands revealed in the magnificence of the mountains, the lakeland valleys, and the desolate moors. Their majesty satisfies our eyes.

We thank you for the work of our hands revealed in the magnificence of skyscrapers, dams, and churches. We pray that their majesty satisfies your eyes.

We thank you for the work of your hands revealed in the excitement of life and death, love and hate, sorrow and joy. Their challenge is stimulating to our hearts and minds.

We thank you for the work of our hands revealed in the excitement of theatre, film, and television. We pray that their challenge is stimulating to our hearts and minds.

ENJOYMENT

THE BEAUTY OF CREATION

84 *Suitable accompanying slides might be; 1) Sea and mountains together, perhaps with a sunset 2) surf on rocks 3) distant hills over a village 4) close-up of a flower. This prayer could be read slowly over gentle music.*

Lord God,
it would have been so easy to create the world according to mathematical rules; all in straight lines. Everywhere we look we see evidence of your love.

Just look at the sea; vast and magnificent. One minute calm and gentle, blue in the sunlight, the next frothing with anger, hurling itself upon the rocks. Never the same, in every mood it shows us some new glory.

Look at the mountains; pure and icy. Now purple in the distance. Now invitingly near, summoning to their cruel peaks, cradling in their gentle valleys; stark in clarity against a cloudless sky, or shrouded in mist. In every mood, they reveal your power.

In the huge vistas of land and sea; in the tiny delicacy of wing or petal; in all the wonder of nature, we see your hand. We are so glad you have made this ever changing, beautiful world for our enjoyment. We revel in it and we praise you, its maker.

THE CITY

85   *Accompanying slides should be of happy city scenes. Any musical accompaniment should be loud and jolly.*

Lord, in our cities there is so much to fill our minds that sometimes we forget you, but we know that you care for all these hurrying, busy people. You are as much in the architecture of the city as in the serene beauty of the countryside.

As we enjoy the rush, help us not to be too rushed to praise you, its ever loving, ever understanding guardian.

HOBBIES

86   Some people like to spend their time outside, chasing a ball, getting all dirty and wet. That's not for me, Lord. I like to stay in, working on my favourite collection. There are lots of people like me, who prefer quieter pursuits, collecting, making models, sewing, gardening or photography.

Everyone has some special interest. Its nice to know, Lord, that we are your special interest, and that you take even better care of me than I do of my hobby.

TEAM GAMES

87   In summer and winter we play our team games together. Cricket, football, hockey, netball and a host of other team games. We need each other to play them. We need each other to win them. Even with a star player, we depend on all the team for support. We must help each other. Lord, help us to see this, not only in sport, but throughout life.

POP CULTURE

88   People sometimes complain with 'What a row!' they say when they hear my style of music. They forget that when they were young and sang about *bicycles made for two* or *yellow submarines*, their parents complained about the row. They too, even forget that their parents complained about their clothes and hair styles. Lord, you understand. Help them to understand that it's the people under the clothes who matter. Help them to tolerate our fashions and help us to understand and tolerate their prejudices. And, when we are old, help us to tolerate and understand our children.

HOSTELS

89   *Slides:—Lone mountain walker; cyclists by river; beach; groups of young people hiking etc.; group in hostel dining room; group in hostel games room.*

Walking alone in the mountains; riding together by the Broads; lazing near the sea or hitching round Europe. A holiday gives us such freedom. Work and exams can be forgotten and, much as we love our families, it is nice sometimes to be just with people of our own age.

Then in the hostel, in the evening, we can laugh and sing. We can talk until the world is put to rights and we can know, as we have seen the glory of your creation in the day, that it is you and you alone, dear Lord, who put us and our world to rights.

ART

90 *This could be read by two voices.*

In our search for knowledge, how good it is, Lord, that thousands of people have been inspired to produce that one picture; that one tune; that one book that speaks just to us.

How good it is too, that you give each of us pleasure in art, not just in receiving, but in producing. Help us to release the beauty, the music and the fine words that are in us, that we may proclaim Thy Glory in our creations.

FOREIGN TRAVEL

91 *Slides: Airport, ferry or hovercraft, Greek beach, Alps, crowded Italian street, multi-racial groups.*

We thank you, Lord, for giving us the means and the wish to travel. Help us, when we see new countries and cultures, to look with unbiased eyes and so to learn that, while places are different, all people are the same: your children and our brothers and sisters.

GENERAL

92 Lord God, our Heavenly Father, we praise, worship and adore you. You have given us so much; a world full of beauty and plenty. You have given us minds to inquire, eyes to behold, bodies to feel. There is so much to enjoy; so much to do. A thousand lifetimes would not be enough to enjoy all there is to be enjoyed here. Yet, you have given us more. In Jesus, you have given us yourself, so that we might live for ever and enjoy the wonders of your Eternal Kingdom.
What a marvellous God you are!

LIVING

LIFE

93 I was going to say: 'Thank you, God, for life',
but that seems feeble.
What words can there be for saying thank you for my
life, for this unearned privilege, this immeasurable gift,
this trust of all that I am and can be?

There is no way I can sum up what I am and what I am
becoming; no way I can count the events and the
experiences and the understandings that have brought
me where I am; no way I can even tell what my
ambitions and expectations are. So how can I offer
thanks?

My life is shared.
Sharing with friends and strangers and those I see as
enemies brings colour and change and excitement into
my life. Sharing discoveries and inventions, actions and
reactions gives textures and taste to every day. So how
can I offer thanks?

I must thank you, loving eternal God, for this life and
for your infinite promise. If I cannot find words, I
must offer my joy and my fears, the beauty and the
ugliness of my life, for you to fashion it into the thanks
you can accept.
Thank you, God,
for life.

GOD'S LOVE

94 *'O God, you are my God . . .your constant love is better than life itself.' Psalm 63.1,3*

You are God, not by my choice but by your own being. I live, not by my deserving but by your creating. Your constant love upholds me, not because I am good but because you are merciful beyond my understanding.

95 Forgive me, O God, for the ways in which I waste my life, the times I put myself at the centre to push you to the edge, the hurt that I do to you in hurting my neighbour. My life, your gift, is to be lived in your way and to your praise; when I forget this, my life is devalued.

96 You show us how to live, Lord Jesus. You had to survive in a hard world, to grow up, get on with family and friends, and get on through all the pressures of life. There was no more safety, and a lot less comfort in your life, than there is for us. Your own experience of human life is part of your love for us now.

97 Please Lord, let us remember your promise of help in our living, and help us to accept it. Help us to share the happiness of life with you just as we want you to share the sad times with us. Be in our ambitions and in our fears in our struggling and in our acceptance. May our living be a way towards knowing you, so that in knowing we may love you and trust you with our lives.

98   How many thousands of millions of lives are there on this planet now, God? And how many millions upon millions have there been in the past? And how can it be that you know about my life, that you care about it? Thank you Lord, that you know and care about your wonderful creation.

99   In all the universe, how many kinds of life are there, God? How is human life so very important, how can it be unique? How many kinds of life have come and gone since you first created?

Jesus, speak to me. Help me to see the love of God in you, making clear the love you have for me, giving value to my life. Jesus, show me again how you turned aside in the important work of your busy life to care for those who had no value in the human scheme of things. You are God's love working in God's world, giving value to the life you share, confirming our creation in your Father's image, our creation for God's own sake.

Help me to live, as you did, to the glory of God, and so to find my life blessed beyond all measure.

100   When we remember that you create life within your world, we remember too that life is more than existence, and life is not for loneliness but for sharing. When we remember our blessings, through which our lives are so enriched, we remember too that there are many whose lives do not rise much above mere existence.

101 We pray, O God, for those who struggle to see the joy that you intend life to bring. Those who live without families or shelter, those who live without food and clothing, those who live without education and security, those who live without health care and the support of others.

If our lives exclude these others, we suffer by being less than we should be. If we set ourselves apart from them, we add to our loneliness and to theirs. If we snatch to ourselves all that we can of what makes life good, and do not seek ways to share it, it will go rotten in our keeping.

102 Help us to live in love for those we know and those we only know about, and to rejoice that you give us such wide horizons. Help us, O God, to work for the true increase of joy and peace in your world of people.

103 *'The Lord God took some soil from the ground and formed man out of it; he breathed life-giving breath into his nostrils and the man began to live.' Genesis 2.7*

I wonder what 'Life' is, God?

It is living that I want to thank you for,
even if I cannot give a definition of what 'Life' is.
Living that gives me a taste of who you are.
Living that gives me a chance to know you.
Living that gives me time to be human.

Life is something to do with love, with growing and knowing.
Help me, O God, to live my life with you.

104 *'I heard the Lord speak to me and I felt his power . . . I saw what looked like four living creatures . . .' Ezekiel 1.3,5*

Where can we find you, God, how can we see something of your Almighty Eternal glory? We cannot look upon you, and our minds cannot comprehend your power. Show yourself to us, O God, as you have always shown yourself to your people. Help us to see you in the life of your creation; turn us away from the images and the attractions of that which is lifeless and uncreative. Draw us to you in the excitement of life, and set us apart from dreariness and stale habit. As we go about the business of our days, open our eyes and ears to know you; in both friend and stranger help us to recognise you; in all the vigour of our youth, let us live as your friends and as those called into your joyful service.

105 *If required, after 'We praise you, O God' a response may be used: 'We praise you, life-giving Creator'.*

In Jesus Christ your life-giving love is shown.
We praise you, O God.
In him everything that lives has its being
and so we live in Christ and through Christ;
he is our life-giver.

106 But he also gives his own life, his love is so great.
We praise you, O God.
So that our lives should not be wasted, useless,
he poured out his life
so that we may enjoy life beyond this life,
eternal life, life with you,
life of joy and peace, life restored by mercy in judgment; in Christ and through Christ our life is given. We praise you O God.

107   *'The first man, Adam, was created a living being; but the*
last Adam is the life-giving spirit.'
1 Corinthians 15.45

Just as it has been from the very beginning, Creator
God, we are living beings because of your power.
If we were not, if you were not, we would be nothing,
but your love is beyond our deserving and beyond our
measuring.

Almighty and Eternal God, to whom all praise, thanks
and obedience belong, you only are God the Creator
and Saviour. In you only may I trust, and to you only
may I offer worship.

By your power and in your mercy, God, bless my life so
that it has purpose and value. May I live to love you and
my neighbour so that people may know your love and
give themselves to you.

THE WAY, THE TRUTH, THE LIFE

108   Out of this turmoil of despair
Lord please hear my humble prayer.
Give me light that I may see
the way that you want me to be.
Let me walk close by your side,
let me know just why you died.
Let me feel your love always.
Let me fill with work the days,
of my allotted span of time.
Let me not commit the crime,
of shirking things I have to do,
As I can do it easier, Lord, with you.
And when the days seem full of strife
I'll remember you are the Way, the Truth, the Life.

MANY ARE CALLED

109   Do you know the right direction
that you are travelling day by day.
Do you think the Lord may be calling you
in a very special way.
What will be your life's vocation?
Pray that it will be revealed.
Perhaps the Lord is calling you,
For your help in the mission fields.
Perhaps you have been specially chosen
the call will come clear and then
when the call you have answered
you will become fishers of men.
So walk in the shadow of God's love
don't stumble through life, don't fall.
But be prepared to accept his decision
be ready to answer the call.

WORLD CRISIS

CULTURE CLASH

110 *List down things you find strange or funny about people from other countries and cultures. Then list down things from your own culture others might find amusing.*

Lord, you created a diverse world for us to live in. A world of different cultures and different peoples. But we are all your children, though we confess that at times we do not show this in our actions.

Father forgive our obstinacy, inflexibility and our cultural biases that insist that we are right and others are wrong, that insist that certain things be said, sung or done, that prohibit some people from knowing you. For you are not white or black not British, American or African. You are the one true God, the Lord of all. Help us O God to overcome our own prejudices, accept different cultures, and strive for your true Kingdom here on earth.

CREATION

111 *Think about the weather, when it rains and when it snows and the times that the sun shines.*

We praise you Lord for the variety of weather you have created.
We pray especially for the countries where rain is a lifeline for the people, the difference between life and death.
Help us Lord, to understand the needs of others,
and not to hide selfishly behind our own desires.
Help us to recognise that what might be an inconvenience for us, is a lifeline for others.

And when we do not always understand some things that happen in this world, help us to remember Lord that you are both the father and mother of creation.
The creator and sustainer of our being.
The Lord of all heaven and earth.

HUNGER

112 *Reflect on the difference between one of your daily meals and the daily ration for many people in poorer countries.*

O God, I've really no idea have I?
I've never really had to go without,
To feel the real pangs of hunger,
To be so hungry that I just cannot eat.

O God, forgive my selfishness and self-centredness
Help me to think more of others and less of myself.
To work and pray for others,
so that I may have less
and that they might have more.

PEACE

113   *Think of situations in our world where there is no peace.*
Reflect on the need for peace, in our own lives, in our
churches and communities, and throughout the world.

Lord Jesus Christ, you are the Prince of Peace,
and you have called us to be peacemakers.
We confess that we have not always followed your
example in seeking solutions for troubled relationships,

> between individuals;
> in families, churches and communities;
> between different faiths and sects;
> and between countries and cultures.

Help us to look to you, and accept you as peacemaker
in our own lives,
so that we can become your peacemakers and seek to
heal broken relationships.
To bring your peace to others and beat our swords into
ploughshares and spears into pruning hooks and so
recreate your Kingdom of peace and light.

HUMAN RIGHTS

114   *Think of situations where the God given rights of people*
have been taken away by earthly powers. Don't forget
situations close at hand! Read Genesis 1.27

Lord Jesus, you came that we might have abundant
life. Life in all its fulness.
We remember those of our world-wide family whose
lives are restricted in any way and so cannot share in
this abundant life.

115   Help us to work for a world of peace and justice, a world free from discrimination, bigotry, apartheid and other abuses of human rights.
A world in which all people are valued and recognised as children of the one true God.

SEX

116   *Heterosexuality, homosexuality, promiscuity, pornography, AIDS, and abortion are those things we read about and talk about but rarely pray about.*
Consider your own God given sexuality.

Our Father, we ask for your guidance as we grow, and develop our own sexuality. For your love and understanding as we try to relate Biblical principles to our own lives.

We ask for your love and compassion for those who are sexually exploited.
Those who are sexually abused.
Those who are discriminated against because of their sex.
Those who suffer as a result of promiscuous relationships.
Those who have contracted AIDS and other sexually transmitted diseases.
Father, help us in our relationships, to reflect your love, understanding and acceptance of us, and your love for others.

GOD'S WAY

117 *Everyone seems to claim the way to solve the world's problems, but there is only one way – God's way.*

Lord Jesus, we know that you are the Way, the Truth and the Life.
Help us to follow you,
and to involve ourselves in this your world.
So that we may see your Kingdom come,
a Kingdom of love and light,
on earth as it is in heaven.
Lord Jesus, when will we realise that there is only one way. Your way.

Lord Jesus, when will we realise that there is only one way. Your way.
When will we realise the radical dimension of your gospel? A gospel that provides guidance and direction for us as we seek to find solutions to the world's great issues and problems? A gospel that challenges and makes demands of us. A gospel that calls us to commitment and involvement.

THE MEDIA

LORD WHERE ARE YOU?

118 *Could be used as a meditation, during which slides could be shown of adverts from magazines etc. or other appropriate images.*

In the jungle of my fantasies
and the dreams of people I'd rather be
Lord, where are you?

Multi-coloured images
flash up for seconds on the TV screen.
That could be me!
In the utopia of my imagination, I am there, it is me,
but . . . Lord, where are you?
For I am here.

The slick, brazen adverts
goad the gullible to spend, spend, spend,
buying an image to suit the ego.
They don't sell us products,
they sell us ourselves.
Whoever we want to be,
airtight, sealed and packaged
in cardboard and sellotape.
Oh! the appeal of the spotless, perfect,
popular and witty
when you're lonely -
and not all you wish you could be.
That's the real me.
So . . . Lord, where are you?
For I am here.

119   I've heard it said that
you are near.
And I've heard it said that
you take me as I am.
If that is so, and you choose
to regard me as so delightful
then all I can say is,
'Please may I see myself
as you do, and not
as I'd like to be?'
For surely you,
who are the Creator of all things,
must know best
and . . .

                                    Lord, where are you?

For I am here.

120   Almighty God,

Thank you that we can understand so much more
of the world because of the mass media.
Thank you that our prayers can be better informed.
Forgive us that we take so much for granted,
including the freedom to speak out
about our beliefs and opinions.

Help us to appreciate the issues which lie behind
oppression, war, famine, poverty, destruction
of your creation.
May we be aware of our responsibilities to work for
your Kingdom.

121 We pray for the media people who research the facts, present the news, compile the programmes and take decisions about the information which is broadcast. We ask that their work may be objective and their motives sincere. We pray for the reporters and cameramen, particularly those overseas in troubled areas, whose very lives are placed in danger in order that we may be better informed. Lord, we rejoice in the power that knowledge can bring but we ask for wisdom and love that our knowledge will be for your purposes and not our own.

122 'YOUTH'

I find it alarming to be told
    I belong to a homogeneous group
whose collective term 'Youth'
    sums up all that is weird in music and dress.
Forgive all those who insist on stereotypes
    and fail to see the individuals
    finding expressions of identity.
Forgive those who create a market for our apparent
    teenage leisure,
    and exploit us as consumers
reputed to have so much money to throw around.
Forgive those who use the media to construct
    false impressions of youth
as noisy, revolutionary, aggressive and unstable.
Sometimes, we are all of these things.
    Sometimes for the good.
Don't they remember what it's like to be young?
But as we struggle to gain recognition
    as human beings,
Forgive us too for so often being
    wrapped up in self.
Please help us to learn from one another with minds
that are open and hearts that are young.

123 Living God, we praise you because you are as much a God of the twentieth century as of any other ages which have gone before.

You are more familiar with our world today than any of us could ever claim to be.

You have given us the ability to create and to discover, and you have watched our developments throughout the generations.

124 Our steps forward Lord are often accompanied by new moral and ethical questions which must be faced, and we need you to help us as we confront these issues. We thank you for our systems of communication, which enable our so-called progress to be understood and explored by a greater number of the population. We ask that the mass media may work for your glory and for the common good rather than for individual or government gain.

125 Thank you for the tremendous enjoyment and learning which can take place because of the media and thank you that even in very remote areas, the feeling of isolation and exclusion can be reduced.

Living God, as we look ahead, may future developments of mass communications, whether local, national or global take shape in a way which is pleasing to you and for the benefit of all.

A TRAGEDY OF NEWS

126 Dear Lord,

the world is indeed a tragic place.
Each day brings along another episode of accident,
natural disaster or human depravity.
>Do we need to know it all
>or is it the news which
>makes the world exist?

Each gory little detail is extracted from the scene
without ceremony or compassion. It is fed to us like
tit-bits thrown out for the birds.
>We are told, we are sensitive consumers.
>We are treated, as gawping voyeurs.

Dear Lord,

help me to make sense of the storms of facts and
speculation. Help me to separate what I ought to know
from what ought to be acknowledged as private.
>Give discretion to those who decide
>whether something should be made known
>for the sake of the general public.

May I not be misled by false impressions or fooled into
taking sides unfairly. Please help me never to throw the
first stones of condemnation, for I am as guilty as any
other.
>May the powers who shape our news
>have respect for human dignity,
>may they have professionalism
>which transcends human greed.

Dear Lord, please accept this prayer now and may we
work to promote good news.

127   Father in Heaven,

we thank you for the technology which allows us to glimpse at the beauty under the sea and at the many different life forms which exist in the depths of the oceans. An insight into a world which was not made solely for human pleasure. Thank you that the wonders of your creation can be represented by film, television, radio and many other forms of media from which we can learn and admire the wonders of your creation.

If used with a youth group or in a similar setting, members could be asked previously to bring along a news story from the TV, radio or press preferably of that day.

128   Lord God,

thank you for your compassion.
May we also have compassion,
and not just for those whom we know.
Thank you for the means to understand a little
of the sorrows and trials which some people are enduring.
Let us always be aware of what is happening outside our own immediate lives and ready to do what we can to further your Kingdom.

We pray especially for . . . (*if there is one news item*)

or

We pray especially for situations and people brought to our attention through the media news . . .
(Either in silence, or praying aloud for the various situations brought as news items,)

129 Lord, may we continue to have compassion as we receive the news, whether from our own country or from overseas.
Open our hearts and minds so that we may know how to pray, for the sake of your Son, Jesus Christ.

FOR TV CELEBRITIES

130 Lord it must be fun to be a TV Celebrity,
to be recognised in the supermarket,
to wear designer T-shirts
and have your hairdresser with you on tour.

It must be fun to know that you give
so much pleasure to so many people
by appearing on TV
or opening a garden fete.

Lord, we thank you for the many 'celebrities'
who bring human company
into lonely lives each night.
We thank you for their talents and entertainment
and pray Lord Jesus, that their own lives may
not be lonely.

POSSESSIONS

131 *'God looked at everything he had made, and he was very pleased . . .' Genesis 1.31*

It is still a good Creation, O God.
Colours and shapes, textures and scents, tastes and sounds are still here for us to enjoy in the things we possess.
Our lives are made easier and more enjoyable every day by the generous love that you poured into the world, and by the things people make for us to use and possess.
This joy, this happiness and satisfaction in having and using is deep in your plan for our living.
And so we thank you: For the things that we use; for the things we treasure and protect and keep; for the things we share with others and things which are our own.
Make our enjoyment holy, O God, of a nature pleasing to you too, an enjoyment which we can offer with our praise and thanksgiving for life in your Creation.

132 *'The twelve disciples went with him, and so did some women . . . who used their own resources to help Jesus . . .' Luke 8.1-3*

How could they do it, Lord?
How could these women in first century Palestine, with all the disadvantage and danger they knew, give up their safety and their possessions to help you in your work?

We find it so hard.

'What's yours is mine, what's mine is my own' we joke to each other; but we really mean it when we say it to you. Every day there is a chance to help you in the way we use our resources.

By sharing, by giving up, by not grabbing at possessions, we could love our neighbour as we love ourselves, and so we could help you in your loving work.

But every day we fail because we do not love you enough, not more than our possessions; we do not trust you enough, not more than the power we think we have.

Lord Jesus, forgive us.

Help us to realise, as the women did so long ago, that only you can make us whole and nothing less than our whole service, with all we are and all we possess, is sufficient response to your love.

133 Eternal God, Father of all and Judge of all the world, we pray for those who are denied their share of the world's resources. You have provided more than enough for all people, with a generosity which flows from your love.

Like a Mother who provides for all her children, you intend us each to share the good things of your world, each to grow in health and strength and enjoyment. Help us Lord, to do your will.

134 When we look around, when we pay attention to the world, we know it is not as you will it to be. So many of your children, our sisters and brothers, have too little even for life, and cannot dream of plenty or luxury. By their standards we have so much, yet we are always being told to want more and to be wasteful. So as we pray for the hungry, the poor, the many millions who have nothing to call their own, help us to see that we must commit ourselves to fair shares within your family, and be held accountable for what we take.

135 *'Sell all you have and give the money to the poor . . .; then come and follow me' Luke 18.18-25*

Lord, it is easy to think that we are excused.

We are not so very wealthy; if we gave up everything we possessed it would not make the slightest difference to the poor of the world. We will surely find it much easier to get into heaven because we are not like the rich man.

But you won't let us get away with that, Lord Jesus. When we set ourselves by your side, and by the disciples who left everything to follow you, we find that we are loaded with possessions, with all sorts of things we want to hang on to.

So do we stand where the rich man stood?
Help us to see if we care more about our treasures than about you. Help us to be honest about where we focus our attention on gathering more things, more treasures about us, or on gathering close to you in obedient love.
And when we see ourselves by the light of your truth, do not let us turn away from you, instead, help us to bring our whole selves and all we have into your Kingdom.

136 *We get so angry with 'things', God.*

We complain when they fail us;
we are hurt when they get in the way,
tripping us up, or bruising us.
It is so easy to lose our temper with things,
to make them carry the burden of blame,
and to excuse our faults through their failings.
But things are just that and no more.

It is when I misuse a thing
that it fails me.
It is when I over value things
that they disappoint me.
It is my carelessness, untidiness
and lack of observation
that produces hurt
not just for me, but for others.

So please forgive me, God,
for trying to escape from my own responsibility,
for my selfish lack of love for other people
in the way I deal with things.
I don't really want to love 'things', Jesus,
but please help me to value them properly
as parts of the world's resources, your creation,
and your gifts placed in my care.

137 Loving creator God, it is sometimes hard to know that
you are here. You tell me that you are eagerly reaching
out for me with love greater than I can measure, but all
around me there is so much that I can measure, and
weigh and price; it gets in the way of your reaching
out.

I can measure how much I have, and how much more
other people seem to have: money, clothes, transport,
food, success . . .

(add anything else that has been talked about recently)

138 I am sure some people have more than their share, more than they really deserve, certainly they have things that I want—surely, God, it ought to be mine, really. Why don't you make sure that I at least get as much as they do Lord?

And when I hear myself complaining to you, I know why I have such a hard time getting to know you. If I fill my eyes and ears, my mind and heart with what I want, in greed because someone else has it, I don't stand much chance of seeing and hearing your love for me.

Forgive my envy, Lord Jesus. Please help me to value truly what I have, and to thank you through the way I use my possessions.

EDUCATION

SPECIAL EDUCATION

139   We pray for people in need of special education because
of mental, physical or emotional handicap. May sufficient resources be made available for their needs, and
may good teachers work with them. They are as much a
part of society as the proudest high-flyers, and so we
pray that they may be so recognised by planners,
experts, and themselves.

140   We pray for people who have special educational needs
because of their families' life-style: for the children of
travelling families—gypsies, armed forces, evangelists,
transport workers; for children in remote areas and in
tiny communities; for children whose parents have
'opted out' of modern society. Grant, O Lord, that the
children are loved and are able to enjoy fully the true
benefits of an education which will best help them in all
their needs.

141   We pray for people who are denied full and fair access
to good educational provision because of their paren-
tage or background, in this and other countries. May
justice and righteousness prevail against those who
would discriminate by race, class, sex or religion, so
that wealth may be rightly allocated for all your children to share your blessings.

142 We pray for people involved in education in your name,
O Christ, whether it be with adults or with children.
For those involved in informal, formal, traditional or
experimental education. Help them to take your teaching as their standard, and your truth as their end, so
that all concerned may be safeguarded from harm done
in a good cause, but rather come to know and to live by
the truth.

143 We pray for people involved in research, that their
work may contribute to human development and
peace. Give them grace, O God, to choose their enquir-
ies with proper regard to society's needs, and to share
their findings in such ways as will best serve your will.
Let not pride nor conceit control them, but may they
find joy and fulfilment in their search and their presen-
tations.

144 *'Can any of you live at bit longer by worrying about it?'*
Matthew 6.27

God, my Creator and Friend, help me to grow.
Yes, I know I cannot add even a centimetre, to my
height or my age, just by wishing it, but I want to grow
in humanity.

145 Help me, please, to learn.
Help me to understand this world you make, how it
should work to your glory and be a source of blessing to
your people.
Help me to seek truth through the opportunities of
study that open around me, so that I come closer to you
and to the people I meet.
Help me to enjoy challenges and tests, seeking the
questions that will open my mind and guide me in your
Way, and meeting them with your companionship.

146   We cannot escape knowledge of good and evil, though we can never become 'as gods'.

Please help me to see how this power of choice calls me to see my learning set within the clasp of your love, so that I grow by your measure and within your will, becoming what you call me to be.

147   *'I am the Lord your God . . . Worship no God but me.'*
Exodus 20.2-3

Forgive me for the times I have set up other gods in competition with you, Lord God.

I have neither carved them in wood or stone, or modelled them in clay, nor have I set before them sacrifices of flesh or cereal.

But I have trusted in them for my salvation: for good reputation and high praise, for hopes of career and promotion and total satisfaction, for a personality and reputation with which I can be pleased.

These are the gods of certificates and grades, the idols of marks and positions, and I have offered them my sacrifice of total priority in time and expectation. I have treated things of true value just on the basis of what I can get from them, as ends in themselves and sources of power. Bring them back into focus, God, as the means by which I become enabled to serve you, offerings which I can bring to you as part of my loving humble worship.

There is none other but you who can be God, Lord Almighty.

Therefore I honour you with all that I am and all that I can become.

148   We pray for our teachers, Lord, and for all concerned with the education system: the people in administration, planning, maintenance and those who provide the books. For the trainers and the inspectors and those who provide the food and all the materials we need.

Bless them all, O Lord, with patience and understanding, and help them to see how we all play our parts in the journey towards that truth which is your gift and your nature.

149   Lord Jesus, after years of walking with you day by day, seeing you heal, hearing you teach, knowing your love, your disciples could still get things wrong. How am I, caught up with all the other study I have to do, to learn your ways?

150   Where you are waiting for me in my books, my lessons, my experiences and my friends, please teach me to recognise you. When you challenge my understanding and interpretation of something learned, help me to share your wisdom.

And when I come to apply the power that knowledge gives me, make me humble and obedient in serving you by loving my neighbours.

151   The thought of a new course is scary, O God.
New people, new rules, new subjects, new timetables and new teachers.
So many people do not seem to understand how worrying a time this is, but you understand everything that happens in life, because you shared the experience of growing up.

Help me to look forward to what will be good.

New people may become new friends.

New subjects may help me to understand more about your world of people—and about myself.

New teachers may be able to work better with me and to stir up a new interest and pleasure in work.

A new course is a step forward in life, where there will always be something new, and something a bit scary, however old I am. Perhaps the teachers and the others are as nervous as I am.

Bless us all, O God.

You will go with me,
just as you will be there already waiting for me.
Help me, O God, to know your presence and to share your strength.

EXAMS

152 Examination time, Lord.

Time for anxieties and fears—and for hopes.

A time when foolish people think that prayer can replace yesterday's work.

So we will not be foolish or insult you; we will not ask you to give us knowledge we could have gained for ourselves.

But we ask for clear minds, for sound memories unspoiled by bad nerves, for the peak of our ability in expressing ourselves so that we do not let ourselves or others down.

You are always with us, loving us, and you know what is important in the minds and in the lives of each of us.

So we offer you this time of crisis, our learning and our plans, for your design.

May the knowledge of your love keep us calm, and may we remember your love for us in years to come.

153 *'Why do you ask me concerning what is good? . . . There is only one who is good.' Matthew 19.17*

We can call you our good Teacher without argument, Jesus, because we know that you are the Christ, God-become-man. You are good as God is good. You are our Teacher, just as you were the Teacher of your disciples who walked with you all those years ago. Teacher, what must we do to be good?

We do not ask you to teach us science or maths; we ask you to teach us truth—for you are the Truth. We do not ask you to teach us geography or history; we ask you to teach us the way—for you are the Way. Biology or language will not be your gifts—you are Life and the Light of the World.

When we live in you we will find that facts become knowledge, information is turned into wisdom. Schooling and training will become an education which makes us more truly human in your likeness; then we can be at your service.

Good teacher, show us how we can gain eternal life.

SUFFERING

SUFFERING

154 Dear Heavenly Father, as a little child trusts her parent, so we should trust you. We sometimes allow little worries and problems to grow out of all proportion, dominating our lives. Help us to lay all our worries and fears before you; to trust you in everything and so to calm our fears and learn to cope with our problems.

FAILURE

155 *Everyone experiences failure at some point in their life.*

You certainly did, Lord Jesus, when men jeered at you and refused to listen. But you knew how to overcome it. You did not brood. You went on to victory. Help us, when confronted with failure, to have the perseverance to try again, if that is right, and the courage to admit when we have not followed your will.

ACCIDENT

156 One minute all is normal. The next, wreckage is scattered everywhere. The very unexpectedness of an accident makes it worse. Lord, when we are faced with tragedy, give us the strength to remain calm, to give help if we are able, and to receive help graciously and patiently.

ILLNESS

157 Lord, there are people whose sicknesses do not leave them easily. Those who feel ill for months on end. Sometimes we get impatient with sick people when they are bad tempered or uninterested. Help us to understand what they are going through; to continue to love; to be patient and compassionate with them.

IN HOSPITAL

158 Lord, when we lie in a hospital bed, we know that the nurses and doctors are doing their best. They are kind and reassuring. But we lie for long periods alone; a prey to a mixture of pain and anxiety; boredom and weakness. It is at this time that we realise our need for you. You alone can give the courage and the patience we need. What a relief it is to know that you are everywhere and that, when our need is greatest, you are close at hand.

BAD DAYS

159 There are days when, from the moment we get up, everything goes wrong.
Machines refuse to work, the weather is foul and people are unhelpful and bad tempered.
On such days, it is so easy to respond by being unhelpful and bad tempered ourselves. Help us, Lord, instead of turning to our ill-humour, to turn to your Holy Spirit to lead us through the irritation of life.

A BROKEN RELATIONSHIP

160 Lord, I really did love *him/her*. I can't understand why *he/she* has gone. One day everything was happy, the next *he/she* wouldn't even see me. What went wrong? I tried so hard. Now I don't know how I feel. Sometimes I hate *him/her* for the way *he/she* has hurt me and then, I long to have *him/her* back. I try to forget *him/her*, but *his/her* face keeps jumping into my mind. I go to places where we went. I see others as happy as we were. I eat food that we enjoyed together. I cannot forget *him/her*.

I want to punish *him/her*; to make *him/her* as unhappy as I am, but I love *him/her*. I'd forgive *him/her* and have *him/her* back tomorrow if only *he/she* would come.

Lord, calm the turmoil in my heart. I know *he/she* will not come back. Help me to remember with thanks the happiness we had together. Help me to forgive *him/her*, even though *he/she* does not seek my forgiveness and bless *him/her*, Lord, wherever *he/she* goes.

A LOST FRIEND

161 *He/she* used to be my best friend at school. We sat together, played together, got into trouble together, did everything together. But I got bored with *him/her*. I found more exiting friends and better things to do.
You needn't tell me, Lord. I know I have done wrong. Please Lord, help me to make amends; to get over this hurt; to say I am sorry and to make friends again.

GUILT

162 If only. What sad little words! Yet we all know the feeling they convey. When it is too late, we think of all the little things we could have done, to say 'I love you' and remember the selfishness we wish was undone. Forgive us, Lord for our neglect of you and of those who are nearest to us. Our feeling of guilt is our punishment. Help us not to be overwhelmed by remorse, but to grow in determination, to remember our Saviour and the feelings of others everyday of our lives.

Reassure us, Lord, that your love and understanding will never fade.

DIVORCE

163 *'O the children are all right. We have explained. They understand. It has all been frightfully civilised, just an amicable parting of the ways.'*

A prayer for the broken down marriage

Lord, help! They don't understand what they are doing to us. They can't see our hearts being torn in two. We love them both. We want them both. We need them both. Lord, stop them being so selfish.

A prayer for the children in the broken home

God feels every pain in your hearts. He listens to your every cry for help. He hears you when your parents hear only their own complaints and their own desires. God knows how much you need and love them both, he will not take sides. God's love seeks to reconcile, comfort and strengthen you.

PRYING

164 *Questions which are well meant can often be hurtful, hitting raw nerves and jarring on weaknesses and secret pains. We struggle to reply, holding the embarrassment and sorrow inside.*

Lord, you do not come asking us impertinent, personal questions. You wait quietly, listening to our innermost secrets when we are ready to tell them. You know our fears and sorrows. You do not have pompous, trite answers. You give strength to face weaknesses and failures; strength to understand and live with our own characters. Please help us to be completely honest and open with ourselves and with you; to remain polite, but non-committal when we are faced with prying questions.
Help us never to ask of others personal questions just for the sake of conversation.

NIGHTMARES

165 Our Father, the night should be calm and peaceful, but there are times when it is full of terror. The subconscious mind summons up pictures of monsters and demons. We are pursued, tortured, devoured, humiliated. We wake panting, covered in sweat; the sheets crumpled and damp and the fear still half on us. Then, our Father, may our first waking breath be to call your name. For we know that no demon, real or imagined, can stand against the God who loves us and saves us.

DEATH

166 *'O death, where is thy sting?*
O grave, where is thy victory?'
1 Corinthians 15.55

Lord, death does seem so final.
People we knew and loved; people who were so full of
life, so active, are suddenly still.
There is no word from them; no movement.

The disciples must have felt as lost and helpless as we
do in the presence of death when they saw your
tortured body on the cross. They were very fortunate.
Within three days, they saw you alive and glorious.
Their faith was made. May we, Lord, when we see
death, receive the same assurance as they. May we
know that, because you live, all who trust in you come
through death to live in the vividness of your glory.

DEATH OF A FRIEND

167 *It is a shock when a friend dies. We miss them. We grieve
for them and we realise that we, too, are mortal.*

Death is the one certainty; the one inescapable terror.
Or so it was , Lord Jesus, before you came. You have
broken its power for ever. You love life. You give life.
We miss our friend. We may fear the manner of our
dying, but we have no reason to fear death.
You have conquered it. By your sacrifice, you have
opened the gate of Heaven. Through you, the friend
who we miss, and everyone of us, has the assurance of
full, glorious life for ever. We praise you, Lord Jesus,
for the victory of life.

THE DEATH OF A CHILD

168 *A child so small and trusting, with so much to give. Why did this child have to die?*

Men have asked why since time began. We cannot understand and, God forgive us, we cannot help but protest. But one thing we can understand. You, our God, are a loving God. This is not a little child lost. It is a little child even more full of life in the house of the Heavenly Father; a child who will never want for love and care. And we know that there is only one who can sustain the parents in their grief. You, Lord, share their suffering and bear it with them. You give strength.

Lord, we ask that when we meet such tragedy, you will sustain us and hold our faith firm, that we may know that suffering is finite, while the bliss of your presence is infinite.

JEALOUSY

169 Of all sins, none is more mean and vicious than jealousy. Carping, cringing, creeping, whining, it seeks to harm for no reason. 'Why should *he/she* have what I haven't got?', it complains. It festers and schemes, bringing low the deserving. It masquerades as virtue, telling tales to drag down the innocent. It wheedles, flatters, slanders, slays. It destroys friendship and breeds suspicion. It is hateful, yet it traps us so easily, telling us that we are merely defending our rights, standing up for the weak or feeling righteous resentment.

Lord, help us not to deceive ourselves, but to recognise jealousy. Then, when it enters our hearts, to stamp on it as quickly as we would stamp on any repulsive, poisonous creature.

EMBARRASSMENT

170 It is so silly. To be sitting in a room and suddenly feel that every eye is on you. To feel sudden warmth. To know that your face is changing colour. To pretend to sneeze to hide it. To hear some unfeeling person say 'Ha! Ha! she's blushing!'

It is so silly , but so unpleasant. Dear, understanding Father, in your loving kindness, you can feel with us when all we want to do is run from the room and hide. Help us not to hide, but grow in confidence, ready to look all men in the eye as we do your will.

ON ANSWERED PRAYER

171 Listen to that still quiet voice
the Lord is very near.
Listen for that still quiet voice
and you will surely hear,
the answer to that problem,
you tried to battle through.
Just listen very quietly
he's speaking just to for you.
He wants to know your troubles
he really wants to know.
And if you'll only let him
great mercy he will show.
So without any doubting
just take him at his word
he listens very carefully
you can be quite sure he heard.

Be still and know that I am God.

HOLY SPIRIT

172   Holy Spirit, three in one,
Holy Spirit, thy will be done.
Descend on us as day by day,
We do our best to try to pray.
In earnestness we come to thee,
dear Lord from all sins set us free.
And make our hearts and minds thine own.
As we worship around thy Heavenly throne.

Give us that peace the world cannot give.
Let us, Lord, just for you live.
To praise and honour and glorify.
So set your seal and hear our cry,
and in the end we'll surely sing
'death indeed where is your sting?'